ALL THE POSSIBLE BODIES

ALL THE POSSIBLE BODIES
POEMS

IAIN HALEY POLLOCK

ALICE JAMES BOOKS
New Gloucester, ME
alicejamesbooks.org

© 2025 by Iain Haley Pollock
All rights reserved
Printed in the United States

10 9 8 7 6 5 4 3 2 1

Alice James Books are published by Alice James Poetry Cooperative, Inc.

Alice James Books
Auburn Hall
60 Pineland Drive, Suite 206
New Gloucester, ME 04260
www.alicejamesbooks.org

Library of Congress Cataloging-in-Publication Data

Names: Pollock, Iain Haley, author.
Title: All the possible bodies : poems / Iain Haley Pollock.
Other titles: All the possible bodies (Compilation)
Description: New Gloucester, Maine : Alice James Books, 2025.
Identifiers: LCCN 2025006526 (print) | LCCN 2025006527 (ebook)
   ISBN 9781949944907 (trade paperback) | ISBN 9781949944488 (epub)
Subjects: LCGFT: Poetry.
Classification: LCC PS3616.O5696 A78 2025 (print) | LCC PS3616.O5696 (ebook)
   DDC 811/.6—dc23/eng/20250325
LC record available at https://lccn.loc.gov/2025006526
LC ebook record available at https://lccn.loc.gov/2025006527

Alice James Books gratefully acknowledges support from individual donors, private foundations, the National Endowment for the Arts, and the Poetry Foundation (https://www.poetryfoundation.org).

Cover: "Eakins Hand" by Samuel Murray (c. 1894). Hirshhorn Museum and Sculpture Garden, Smithsonian Institution, Washington, DC, Gift of Joseph H. Hirshhorn, 1966

CONTENTS

1. AMERICA,
A Black Mother's Child Considers His Lost Dream of Immortality {3
Metaphysics with Poppies {5
Weighing Death by Patricide (on the Old Croton Aqueduct Trail) {8
All the Possible Bodies {11

2. IS YOU IS
These Moral Currents Cut {15
Lady Soul {17
Deep Down, Every Sinner {18
Selfhood Among Nationhood: Mythic Imperatives {20
Is You Is, or Is You Ain't? (An Answer Becomes a Set of Further
    Questions) {22
Romanticized Portrait of My Self-Loathing as the Poleman in Eakins's
    Rail Shooting on the Delaware, Also Known as *Will Schuster and Blackman
    Going Shooting* (1876) {26
Abrupt Edge {28

3. OF MARKS & LACKS {29

4. ARTIFACTS
Turn, hell-hound, turn! {45
Horace Silver Hexagonal Blues {47
Subject of My Desire (In Which You Do Not Figure) {48
Artifacts {49
[Weather of summer and weekend blur] {51
Not a Prayerful Kneeling (for John Lewis) {53
for I think upon the price of my redemption {57
On a Different Day {59

5. MYTHOLOGIES OF THE SUBURBS
These and all else were to me the same as they are to you {63
The Dismantling of Moscow's Bells {66
Lessons Ending in Allegheny Plum {68

Notes Toward My Younger Boy's Possible Biographies of Me {69
On Black Quarterbacks & Dogfights in Virginia Woods {71
Ward Pound Ridge {72
Mythologies of the Suburbs {73
In Some America / a Gun {75

6. RENDERS ITSELF VISIBLE IN MY BODY
Heron and Light at the Croton River {79
Frequency & Amplitude: the Child / Sing {80
Danse Printemps et Quarantaine {81

Notes on the Poems {85
Acknowledgments {87

FOR TERRENCE D. WILLIAMS & DAVID B. EYE

1. AMERICA,

A BLACK MOTHER'S CHILD CONSIDERS HIS LOST DREAM OF IMMORTALITY

I.
What was she hoping I'd learn? What lessons
when my mother, who taught Greek
at the college on the hill, read their old stories
to me? To be ready one night for hooded snakes
to crawl into my cradle? To leave a trail of twine
behind me as I walked the labyrinthine corridors
of my country? Not to raise the wrong sail
whenever I came home to her? Not to dive
as the swan and plummet into a woman bathing
in the seclusion of high reeds, not to be the shock
and awe of white wings? For me though, the truth
in the myth was this: power transforms
into life, and life forever. And when my mother
was finished, all I wanted was to live
as those changing but unchanging gods.

II.
The White man who taught me Greek
hated me. He thought I was lazy. I admit
that I often slept through his morning class,
often stumbled through his translations as a boar
through deep, sudden snow. My mother cried when
she left me in the parking lot of that place. Cried
harder than I'd seen since the week after her father
died. I think she had learned that no Black mother
can save her children. Save them, as you have proven
(and are still proving), America, from your primitive,
bullhorned violence. And so, more days than not,
her son stood beside an aluminum keg, fermenting
himself, pouring into his gullet a river,
not of forgetfulness, but of an urgent forgetting.

III.
My mother wanted to learn Latin on her way
to Greek, but the teachers had her pegged
to cook and sew. Short but thickset,
the school's own former football hero, her father
traded on his glory, the scars earned for it,
on his hobbled knees, the slight slur of his speech
to demand a place for her in a room of primers
and chalkboards. They thought she should scurry
about the rooms of your house, America, picking up
what you had dropped. But she overcame to stand
at the front of a room, professor of language
and myth. I told a version of this story to Black children
at a school in Philadelphia. When I came to the end—
my mother teaching Greek at the college on the hill—
they rose from their chairs and applauded her
through the proxy of me. I think now I lied to them.
Lied to them while standing in a room across town
from where you firebombed a city block to save
yourself. America, you have eaten your children
to keep your place on the honeyed mountaintop.
If you have not already, you will consume these children
too. And still you will come, with wild, ravenous hunger,
for more. And why do you keep doing what you do?
And what will you do one day when, instead of a child,
you swallow a stone?

METAPHYSICS WITH POPPIES

I can't understand, after years of reading, the relevance
of metaphysics. How does it account for the wants of my mind

breaking apart my body? I prefer to think of poppies,
the variety fated to bloom blood-red. Or, of planting poppies,

any flowers in truth—how they come to us in plastic pots; how
after we shovel them a place in the earth, we extract

the flowers from their vessels; how while we lower them down
into their potting hole, ganglionated roots and the dirt compacted

around those roots retain the container's shape. I am interested
in the shape of things. Is that the relevance of metaphysics?

You know I'm hiding again, don't you? Still the boy
between the cedar and the wedge of stone wall where, lying flat,

he cannot be seen from the first house his parents ever owned.
I am hiding because I am tired of broken promises,

my country's and my own. I thought we promised never again
to clothe bodies, especially of children, in chain link.

But here we are. And me, I promised to jettison the anger
that howls away at those, especially the children, I mean to keep

closest to me. But here we are, anger not exorcized,
stashed instead on a high shelf, loaded and with the safety off.

I need that anger—brandishing it I feel most electric and alive.
That's not quite it, but I cannot make the story only about me:

we would not let a woman and a man and their sons
walk across a bridge. Or, if we had, when they arrived,

we would have outfitted the boys in that broken promise
of fence. I can't understand what we feared. Maybe

that we'd fall out of love with a country that never was
as we imagined it? Maybe that we'd fall out of love

with ourselves? The sons gathered between the woman
and the man, the four hitched arms and waded

into the water we've decided separates that place from
this place. As the four experienced it, swollen and churning

with a confluence of spring rain, the river was both abstract
and real. You know the resolution: water suddenly high,

wrench of undercurrent, the boys drowned. The first son
washed into a backwater matted green with reeds eroded

out of their soil. Where, downstream and returned
to the other side, the second son floated to something like rest,

soda cans bobbed with him in the shallows. As the mother
and the father could not, I am afraid that I cannot protect

my children. I use anger to keep myself, and them, alive.
This is wrong. I am wrong also to make the story of the woman

and the man and their sons about me. I made a different promise
never to masquerade in stories not my own. But I hid behind them,

their story, as I hid behind metaphysics, poppies, anger, a cedar,
and fear. I hope it matters, although I suspect it doesn't,

that I broke this promise in good faith: their story
is not my story, but if I don't see myself in them—the four

in the water and not on the bridge—what do I stand
in relation to? what are my properties? what shape am I in?

WEIGHING DEATH BY PATRICIDE
(ON THE OLD CROTON AQUEDUCT TRAIL)

When, this spring, the virus shut us in,
the older boy and I
wore each other mean—
the friction of father and son heightened

by all around us the spidering sense
of sickness. I was glad the bitterness
between us went unseen
behind our house's heavy, paneled door.

Summer today, and the city and towns here
less ravaged, we walk again
in the open world. The older boy
has broken off the homeward

hike from the berm where
the old aqueduct once ran.
He has climbed onto a white-hickory trunk
fallen by the trail's side and walked its length

to stand near the root ball,
deracinated and dangling in the air.
Balancing, he spears
a sharp-pronged stick

into the tree's decomposition,
each jab kicking up
a spray of softened wood.
The younger boy stays closer

to the trail and me, content
to peel away thick swaths

of diamond-furrowed bark.
He beams in triumph as he holds up

larger and larger strips, trophies
for me to see. Should I be disturbed
by their destruction? Their joy in it? Their zeal?
These last few weeks they've been scaring me.

In their waking dreams of patricide,
I've died a dozen gory deaths: every stick
a bayonet to thrust into my back,
every thumb the hammer to a six-shooter unloading

its cylinders into my chest, every upper-story window
an invitation to my body's forced fall,
every rock a grenade to send shrapnel
under my skin in search of organ

and bone. I'm grateful, in this moment,
to let the downed white hickory entertain
their latent violence. While the older boy's head
stays lowered and he stabs at the trunk,

the younger trots my way pinching a millipede.
He leads me to where he found it—
a slow riot of arthropods crawling
on the hickory's exposed wood, feeding there

on fungi, first cause of this decay.
I should not fear a sharp death,
homemade knives shivved
into a heaving sack of lung.

I should fear some death more like this:
a boy turned from me
who won't turn back
while the thousand-footed failings

I never wanted seen
work steadily
under the bark
and ravage me away.

ALL THE POSSIBLE BODIES

My alcoholic grandfather couldn't hold his money
& passed a bad check. Hampton / Virginia / after *Brown
v. Board* but before Selma's Bloody Sunday. After
my grandmother died but before he moved the family
North / back to the town of his birth. My mother saw
her father cuffed & dragged from the house. The next
day / by some miracle she never understood /
he came home.
    Had he looked at the officers wrong /
acted wrong / spoken wrong / been too familiar / been
a few inches taller / been deeper voiced or darker skinned
& for this had he caught a knee that night to the neck
& not returned / perhaps my mother / needing to stay home
& raise Aunt Joan & Uncle Keith / would have skipped
college. Had she skipped college / perhaps she would not
have gone for a Ph.D. Had she not gone for a Ph.D. /
perhaps she would not have met my father. Had she
not met my father / perhaps I would not be here /
perhaps the boys sleeping upstairs from me now
would not be here.

When you spend 8 minutes & 46 seconds / with your knee /
on another man's neck /
      you block not just the passage
of air / into his body / but block air into all the possible
bodies / dependent on that man /
& his neck / to breathe / breathe / breathe /
breathe / breathe—

2. IS YOU IS

THESE MORAL CURRENTS CUT

Half my bad childhood racial memories happened
at middle-school dances. The blond boy who snatched
the fresh Malcolm X hat off my head, threw it down
into a dance floor mess of fruit punch & gritty footprints,
& told me *you're not black—stop pretending*. (Entire careers
made of upholding that line when we refuse to run patrol
for them.) At another dance, I was ringed by leering
white faces that belted out, *It don't matter if you're black*

or white. I wasn't sure what those faces meant, but I knew
they meant to hurt. I've never held that lyric against Michael
Jackson. I do find, though, listening to his old albums,
those Jackson 5 records with cuts like "Never Can Say
Goodbye," has gotten hard. These days I know how that story
ends: the descent into dysmorphic madness, the predatory

doors bolted & shut behind boys, one stolen childhood
thieving another. My better angels think it's wrong
to separate the art from the artist. I hated learning
Pound in school when we all knew he was a fascist
& anti-Semite. He should have stayed locked
in the gorilla cage of his hate. But then I admit Miles Davis
has lodged brass notes irrevocably under my fifth rib,
& some of those notes he bent while blacking & bluing

Cicely Tyson. (Cicely goddamn Tyson . . .) & on the night MJ
died, I danced to his music in a circle of dancers until my shirt
was sweat-stuck to my chest, until I stank with grief.
I didn't know then all that disgusts me now—the doors,
the boys—but the hard truth is: if the King of Pop died today,
I don't think I could stop myself from letting hips sway

to music that, especially in the writhing all-night body rock
of a house party but even in my mother's halting soprano,
pushes past *joy* to *abandon*. These moral currents cut the other
way too: the blond boy who snatched the X hat off my head,
when a young man, walked into a gas-station store to find a woman
being beaten by her boyfriend & when the blond boy went to stop
him, the boyfriend ignited a lighter & touched it to the boy's shirt,
which burned until it curled into a sneer & then stuck to his white skin.

LADY SOUL

How easy, driving the White Mountains—
sundown, three beers deep—to hold
the wheel steady and become a tangent,

jump the banked asphalt, rip through
the guardrail, to give over to gravity,
let it drag you down into a birch trunk
or a glacial erratic's weathered granite.

They'd blame the wreck on alcohol or
your ignorance of the road or the severity
of the curve.
                    But before you left the bar
in Plymouth, you queued her on the car stereo,
a combustion internal and holy revving in her voice.

As you drive, sunset hazes around the peaks,
and she's singing—*people   get ready*—
and you follow her.
                  When you pull the car
beside the house where you'll spend the night,
your tires spray gravel against the vinyl siding.

And next morning, you wake to dawn light
blocked by curtains into shifting shadow.
                                        Light
blocked but there and rippling into the room
when the still-cool summer morning sets the curtains
to sway.
        How close you came to not being
in that sunlight, sunlight resinous and rippling

and rippling and rippling and there.

DEEP DOWN, EVERY SINNER

The subject of the dream is the dreamer.
—Toni Morrison

The night & the tree were always & never about us.
    We could have been any bodies a shade
darker than destiny manifest. & the crime
    alleged could have been real

or imagined: the rape by the muddy riverbank,
    or the phantom wolf whistle, the glance seen
to linger like a stain no washing scrubs out.
    Death came long before our neck bones

snapped like so much deadfall beneath a boot's
    heel, long before the rope's rough sisal
collapsed our windpipes. The precise moment
    of our dying was the hour they turned

our dark bodies into sign & signifier for the savage
    instinct & base desire they dreamed lurking
at the center of them. You see it best
    when we let force of habit take over & leave

ourselves invisible. With us gone, all that exists
    beyond the spare, singular trunk
of the hanging tree is the vacuous night sky,
    starless in the camera's gaze. You see it too

in them who gathered to watch us made
    human effigy of the breached Commandments
they could not confess. How many of them
    look back toward the camera? Deep down,

every sinner wants his sin seen. We did not need
    to be there for this laying bare. But we were,
indelibly. The fiction could not happen without us,
    nor waking from fiction into the delusional

sunlight of their daily lives. We were there.
    We are here. Real & imagined, as the creaking
of boughs under an unseen weight, under a wind unseen
    but felt along the creased & nervous terrain of the skin.

SELFHOOD AMONG NATIONHOOD: MYTHIC IMPERATIVES

To survive,
I am doing what my country
has asked: making
a myth of the land
and of the self.
The country myth
was cradle-born,
sung into us
while we slept.
My own myth:
I will not tell it
plainly. Or, I cannot:
who can discern
the stories we spin
to stay alive
from the real—
solid core at which
we never quite arrive?
I will keep doing
what my country
has asked me to do.
Does it matter
that the land
is never our own?
That my self, buffeted
in the wind of obligation,
is never quite my own?
I will live the myths I know
by heart and those
I stumble through.
To survive,
I will hew to them,
myth of country,
myth of self,

even as the feral claws
of the real gouge
at the basswood
in our mask.
My country has asked,
and I have answered,
and I do not know
what else to do.
If the myth
flies from me,
out of my sight,
an obscure river bird—
heron, egret, osprey—
skimming the surface
until it becomes the water
and is gone to the eye,
what of these borders,
what of this body
will I have left?

IS YOU IS, OR IS YOU AIN'T? (AN ANSWER BECOMES A SET OF FURTHER QUESTIONS)

What are you? you have asked. You are either a male student whom I know but do not teach and whose parents avoid racial conversation at the dinner table, or a woman in a Houston bar who has run her fingers through my dreads without asking permission. Whoever you happen to be, please clarify your question: are you asking in the existential or the racial sense? My knee-jerk existential answer is: I am a human. I am a human constituted of the anatomical-emotional-physiological-historical-genetic-cultural-psychological-social complexity of our species. This human status

renders a complete response to your question *What are you?* (or more properly *Who are you?*) so intricate and expansive as to make the question functionally unanswerable in the time our encounter—which we both want to be as brief and casual as possible—allows. I'm willing to wager, however, that you're asking option two: the racial question. And I'll double down that you're asking from within the narrow confines of an American construction that carries the racial residue no salt air could scour from hulls of conquistadors' and colonists' Atlantic crossings, such that your question bears a Victorian, at best, conception of race as its subtext. In that case, trying for a quick exit from the conversation, I'll say that as the issue of a White father and a Black mother, I am a *mulatto*. (Although having seen the genetic data from my mother's mitochondrial mothers, I am something closer to a *quadroon*, but I would have to explain this term to you, extending our chat longer than either of us desires, so I'll leave my answer at the degrading and zoological original—part man, part pack animal.) To move hypothetically forward in racial time, if you were asking your question

from a place of conscious Blackness, a latter-day *Négritude*, I would answer, *My momma's Black as your momma* (which may or may not be entirely true) to create an authenticity that would, with any luck, bind me to you and evolve into a sense of belonging such that I'd have some soft place to rest my head in this dirt-hard, fractured little America of ours. This scenario is not to be though—whoever you are, you most decidedly do not speak from a place of conscious Blackness. Of course, I could try my most honest answer: in the history of recorded ideas and migrating peoples, no one has invented a category that precisely defines *What*, in your idiom, I am. (The same could be said for you, I'm sure, had we time and want enough to wade into your genetic pool.) If the world continues as it does to change and stay the same, I do not in my lifetime predict success in this definitional endeavor and particularly not star-spangled success. By pointing to the paucity of categories precise in their definition of me, I do not reject love for my mitochondrial mothers, stolen as they were from their Gold Coast homes, shipped as they were across a body of water stretching farther than they

imagined a body could stretch, enslaved as they were in Spotsylvania County, Virginia, for the purpose of producing Orinoco tobacco. Nor do I reject love for my father's Englishness (although were you and I desiring to engage for longer, we could scope the purity of this Englishness: historical records and family lore suggest 19th-century Pollock forebears were forced from the Scottish Highlands during the Clearances while the reddish tint of my father's beard suggests a Viking in the woodpile—the colonizer and colonized again rehearsing their psychodrama within the double-helix of me). *What am I?* I am a whole that is equal and unequal to the sum of his parts. A liquid in a solid system. The undetected spectrum floating between fixed poles of a binary. I'm something while not being anything that humans, especially American humans, can figure out. Picking up social cues, the clock has wound down on our encounter, and you are, as I am, eager to go our separate ways—you're late to Geometry or your boyfriend waits with a gin and tonic—but my ambiguity of speech and person might have threatened you, so let me retreat into civility and ask: *Did I answer your question?*

ROMANTICIZED PORTRAIT OF MY SELF-LOATHING AS THE POLEMAN IN EAKINS'S *RAIL SHOOTING ON THE DELAWARE*, ALSO KNOWN AS *WILL SCHUSTER AND BLACKMAN GOING SHOOTING* (1876)

A cruel mirror, mud-dark water reflects the blithe clouds
from which these railbirds plummet when, a blur & rush
of wing, Schuster snaps them out of the sky.
Behind Schuster his poleman, wearing a jockey hat
& sleeves rolled up his taut arms, holds still & steady their punt
pulled in close to marsh reeds along the Delaware.

If I were the poleman, I would not have craned
to see around Schuster & his red shirt, to witness his target
become a small explosion of feathers before it fell
into open river, a rock dropped off a creek bridge
by a boy's hand. Or, if I were he, I would have
pretended to care if Schuster clipped the rail while I wondered
about his fragile balance, wondered if, with Schuster lost
in sighting the bird, if I could have gotten away with it.

If I were he, could I have swept Schuster's legs, my pole
buckling the backs of the knees, the man plunking
into the marsh-slop, hunter turned quarry? Could I have
knocked his skull then pinned him in the muck
until the thrashing stopped? The more his flailing soaked
the twill of my trousers the better— I could have said: *When*
the punt tipped, he fell & cracked *his head on the edge, then slipped*
overboard. I lay across the boat *& leaned out after him*
but couldn't get him to come to, *couldn't lift him above the water*
& onto the stern. I tried to save *Mister Schuster, Mister Schuster*
who all day had been so good *& kind to me. I should've*
done better, should've woke him up or *pulled him out or kept the boat*
steadier. I should've saved *Mister Schuster, who must live in a big*
Philadelphia house built *on a gold brick foundation,*
with a big Philadelphia family. Should've *saved him.*

But I am not he. & even he is not he: a fiction, *Blackman*,
a cipher for Eakins—& me —a vessel filled with our ideas
of order. Even if he were & I were he, I would still be I.
I would never have tried to spill Schuster over the side,
dislodge him from his perch & down to where reeds
grab root in rank mud. I would've confirmed him, made him
feel the big man he knew himself to be, would've praised
the trueness of his aim: *Best shot I've ever seen & I've been doing this*
a long time—long time. When he missed, I would've held
the blame, said: *Sorry for jostling* *the boat, sir, just when you were*
pulling the trigger. To his every word, I would've nodded
& nodded & nodded, would've agreed his every claim
was right even when I thought they were wrong as saying
water flows away from the sea & back up to the mountaintop.
I would only have done, could only have done as I imagine
the poleman did: pilot Schuster around that marshland,
help gather up his killed fowl, then steer him back to Fairton.

All the while my hate for Schuster would've grown
& grown—that house on gold bricks, that voice ringing
like so many silver coins when he tells me to push here,
push there, that treasure trove giving him this lode of time
to stand out in Cohansey backwater wearing a shameless red shirt
& blasting away at little, no-meat birds—grown & grown
my hate for Schuster, cruel mirror shining back
my hate for me,
for my self,

my shuffling,
    nodding,
        eyes-cast-down self,
my ego-propping,
    yes-sirring,
        holding-the-boat-steady self.

ABRUPT EDGE

Out of thicket
and cover, a sparrow
darts for seed spilled
in high, browning grass,
seed to crack and
throat down later
in the imagined
safety of nest. The red-tail
dives hard, sharp shins,
talons thrust, violent and
awkward with velocity. Dives
until, too late, the sparrow
hears the menacing wind
of descent in mottled feathers.
Not talons, but blunt force
of impact crushes bone
and organ. Knocks hunger
and what remains of song
from a small, hollowed
body too enraptured
by orange dusk,
by the promise
of day's last seed,
a body too ignorant
of sky and above
to have been afraid.

3. OF MARKS & LACKS

Brackets are an aesthetic gesture toward the papyrological event rather than an accurate record of it . . . brackets imply a free space of imaginal adventure.

—Anne Carson

someone will remember us
              I say
                      even in another time

—Sappho, fragment 147, trans. Anne Carson

I.) amid the weeks[   ]isolation,[
with my boys: hurtling[
                              ]downhill[
creek water, the younger in pursuit of the older—[
                ]the older who knows[
                                    ]he must be
caught,[   ]a defense
]
]
graceful[   ]all the starkness[
                ]reflecting[
sun[   ]a contrast[   ]ungreen
        ]coming into leaf.[
all day[   ]the boys indoors,[   ]on letters and
numbers[   ]late afternoon[   ]behind the
        ]fence, we'll throw a soft-hearted baseball[
        ]build forts in the friable leftovers of last summer's
sandbox, late afternoon when the sun will slant into our hillside
windows at its usual acute angles[
                ]i have not told them how[
many are dead[   ]when the older asked[
        ]faster than they should down the gorge[
        ]over time, into the bedrock marble.[
                ]the end of our walk,[
            ]i stop before i reach them and watch[
        ]under an arch, dogleg right, and flow[
            ]i've seen where this creek spills[
        ]just north of the station[
        ]how it wends from here to there, i'm not certain, and
today i wonder if[
]

II.) amid the weeks of illness and isolation: thrust of shovel
blade, my hands in the dirt, the beauty of new[
]
]
]
                                        ]but the
tendrils of english ivy scaling[
]
]
]
]
]
]
]
]
]
]
                        ]remnants, limp as
strangled snakes, into last autumn's leaf fall. a small, protective killing[
]
                                        ]as these
laurels grow, some people will see them as salvation, the
white-flowered ecstasy of the perennial. some people,[
                        ]bloom, not me.

                ]the weeks of[
]
]
]
]
who wait for food six feet from the bodies[
]
      ]—a long line but not desperate. and to occupy me:
the norway and silver maples on the surrounding ridges
                ]their red swell all the more vivid against
a sky that glowers[
]
the trees allow clear[
]
                                        ]to the lone
      ]balanced on the hillside[
]
]
      ]looking over[
time to time[
]
]
                ]an eroding tree bed, its mulch washed
away over the winter[
the car,[
                                        ]my eyes[
                        ]the gloves, the mask, the
                                ]weeks of illness[
            ]stay fixed[   ]how long before nature
runs its course,[
]
                        ]comes sliding, in a sudden
  thunder, down the slope?

IV.) amid[
                    ]porch[
red, hardbound[   ]too young to
decipher[   ]rusted, strident[
]
]
                                        ]before this
spring[   ]nature's indifference[   ]granite
                                        ]slab snow
intransigent in[   ]descent. but today
                    ]my insignificance is not distant
and sublime:[   ]prophesy warmer
days[   ]surge[
radiant yellow[
     ]the few[   ]burgeon[   ]pink and
]
     ]behind shut doors[   ]bide their slow
quarantine, while down river,[
               ]a discordance[
               rasping to[   ]hard-set[

                        ]isolation, i
deliver[
            ]groceries—[
                  ]shut down—[   ]then run[
back on a steep trail[   ]croton river.[
gorge, water sounds its bass[
heavy rain streams toward the broader hudson and[
flow. on my way back[   ]black
vultures[
come to perch in a spectral[
above the gorge this early[   ]they shouldn't[
the vultures.[
but warmer days have pulled their range[
riverine hills they scavenge for roadkill[
rancid forms of [   ]no interest in me—i am[
and moving for now—but tuck beak to feathered[
and wait for what carrion may come[

VI.) on hart island, city workers[   ]digging[
the unclaimed dead. can i be happy[
here i am: taking joy in stooping with[   ]the porch
and potting boston ferns into[   ]baskets, in the
       ]boy hunched over his comics,[   ]younger boy at
              ]paint into a muddy[
         ]brothers yawping with[   ]sticks[
                ]drop their yellow and the lilac
              ]neighbors and friends will die
                ]in their lungs. i know[
and still, because i have been[   ]the weeks of illness and
isolation, i cannot choke back this happiness: i love being among
the ordinary[   ]and alive.

VII.) amid the weeks of illness[
arrive more autumnal[
crow wings and flaps, west and north[
hudson, brown now with soil eroded[
this bird cannot fly as it should, as the crow flies. but rolls
      ]in patterns of[   ]currents, patterns and
      ]discernible slashing through[
greenly, luxuriantly unfurled[
         ]i cannot—at the high,[
         ]bewildered flight—i cannot[

VIII.) amid the weeks of illness and isolation[
 ]nightly into our bed, climbs over the escarpment of
his mother, and wedges himself[
]
turning spring, light not yet limning[
gather him across my forearms, blunder down the hall,
 ]back into his bed. wrapped[
 ]he'd shut-eye[
 ]return to our room and mattress. by early summer,
 ]let him lie with us,[
 ]flailing nights, he'd
 ]frame perpendicular to ours,[
 ]his mother's waist, his feet slung
 ]bodies a crude[ ]*h*
]
 ]the weight[
 ]down onto my socket and joint[
 ]awake.
 ]trundle and horn-blare[
 ]trains[ ]near-empty cars into the proud but
intubated city.

    ]illness and isolation, this petty
disaster[
]
                  ]swells under the microscope of
our always-togetherness.[
]
]
]
    ]outage source: the[
mockernut branch snapped[
       ]live wire hit the road, all pock and warp,
the bitumen[   ]superheated,
bubbled back to oil, then cooled with[
    ]distortion and flow.[
]
    ]galvanized[
]
    ]peeking out now of its half burial[
inscrutable[   ], a petty disaster: we in
the dark[   ]rejoined. the lights
]   the road repaired[   ], no sign the
wire was ever[   ]disaster[   ]amid the
weeks of[

]hoops and soap suds[
younger boy twirl fantastic summer[
weeks of illness[   ]the size of my torso
in knobby sphericals and distended tubulars. warped,
                    ]memory given shape and
prismatic[   ]floating, currents of breeze
               ]toward the laurel and[
               ]property line, the neighbor's
               ]dilapidating behind them. floating,
    ]surface tension—under pressure from trapped
                         ]—breaks.[
                  ]the air holds a thin perimeter of
                              ]form. ghost of an
apparition. but then, even this hint[
     ]knows gravity, into the grass and[   ]loam, falls
away.

XI.) opening[
]
]
]
]
                                        ]retains its
fragrance, vaguely floral—lavender? lilac?— the redolence
great aunts wear against their aging. when i left[
                            ]i had a flickering idea
i wouldn't be back[
            ]time is now, and here i am. the calendar still
hangs open to march. outside the window, a paper birch
                                ]and isolation, unruly
across the playground[   ]branches
brushing its slide, cordoned off[
                ]unused this year. no shrieks and
whoops keeping me[   ]no teacher
calling her students back to the classroom. no straggler
having to be coaxed and called again. the bark peels[
                    ]the calendar[   ]will not
unfix itself[   ]a full year[
                    ]me the office air haunts with all
the perfumes[   ]but never noticed enough to
]

XII.) all the time[   ]in the end
    ]a woman[   ]a brick[   ], a man[
               ]each—rattling[
      ]—refused death, respite[
the hunger of days[   ]when i am they, diastolic
heart begging arteries to pay back the blood owed, flaccid lungs
praying for the deliverance of air, i'll regret[
         ]solemn days amid the weeks of[
isolation,[
leaden as a counterweight[
]
]
]
]
want now what is here:[   ]slate of this sky,[
     ]hemlocks,[   ]pasted thick
with nor'easter snow. the raw, deep-set[   ]wind
chirring in the[   ]needles. here,
heavy branches[
threatening to splinter[   ]here,[
                                  ]hardened,
snowbound[   ]here. i want[   ]what is here.

4. ARTIFACTS

TURN, HELL-HOUND, TURN!

First hearing the story of it—Robert Johnson's
midnight-crossroads-hoodoo deal with the Devil—
no way I would have mortgaged my soul to burn

my Blues redder & hotter than any since or before.
I was a boy, back then, who cared about my *rep*.
& my *rep* hinged on acting good, *no matter*,

like adults said, *who was around*. Consorting with him
of horns & pitchfork wouldn't have been good,
size of the prize be damned. Now, I side

with that queen gone wandering crazy: *Hell
is murky*. Sure, most times there's no silt in the river:
I've done good that I knew was good & bad

knowing it was bad. But then, I've done bad trying
to do good & strangest of all, good when I set out
to do bad. Now, I can't see a way to salvation

from this cross-stitch of lonely, dust-licked country
junctions but the Devil. That old goat doles out more mercy
in an hour than God since He first flicked on the lights.

Now, I'd shake on that bargain in the beat of a blue bottle's
wings, would trade my soul & my good name & my rep
for talent without sending the fine print to my lawyer

or hemming & hawing over the non-refundable nature
of the ticket. & I'd settle on that sulfurous offer
with no illusion that talent is happiness, knowing

I'd be trading that maze of good & bad for a labyrinth
of jealous husbands with every chamber of their .38s
loaded up. Of women I two-timed bubbling &

troubling strychnine into my whiskey glass. Of hot grits
blistering my back. Of razor blades under the tongues
of rivals. Of friends easily bought but gone

when trouble calls. Of starless nights of self-doubt
ending in the scalding light of hangover. Of a lifetime
of cash-stuffed envelopes not saving children

from the sting of my absence. I know this, & still
I'd cut my palm & sign that cloven-footed pact
in blood. If up is down, & left is right, & I can't

be good the way my boy-self wanted, why be
common & untalented too? Why not trade this street
of unlocked doors & rhododendron, this refrigerator

humming to save my abundance unspoiled,
this family like a Christmas card's gloss of family,
why not trade all this to have the myth of me

handed down father to son, father to son?
Since I can't be good in this world, why not ink
my autograph to the Devil's dotted line & be great?

HORACE SILVER HEXAGONAL BLUES

Horace Silver's left hand sailing along the ebonies
and ivories has me thinking, though I do not want
to think, about respectability politics. Who knows why?

No, be honest: I've played them all my life,
though not always on purpose. Be honest: same
difference. Whether or not I meant to, I have kept

the honeyed class in their honey. I want to stop
working the 'combs. I want me to live in disrepute. To pick
the corn from between my front teeth with the long nail

of an index finger. To wipe my nose clean with a forearm sleeve.
To throw popcorn and insults into the cinema's dark silence.
To eat every meal with my hands, to tongue the leftover sweet

from my knuckles. That none of this will happen is not
Horace Silver's fault—I did this to myself, let the hive
be spun around me (and did some spinning too), ground

myself with labor until even the most respectable music
sounded like fear. Be honest: all these hours worrying 'combs
and worrying honey wind up with my body losing its scent

of wax, and my kin dragging me out, dropping me
down into some field distant from the hive where I don't
have to work this ordered mess of hexagons no more.

SUBJECT OF MY DESIRE (IN WHICH YOU DO NOT FIGURE)

    Homenaje, *Julio Le Parc (1959)*

I've learned not to trust the composition
of my desire until the longer we live together,

the more you abstract into a monochromatic
geometry: light in our furnace room dissolving

into the shadowed corner we take turns sweeping
clean. A trompe l'oeil of dove flocks and crow murders

playing in the harvest of your irises. Halogen shining
through a dark and diamond fence around the town pool,

fence that, at full-moon midnight in faraway girlhood,
you're still trying to scale. The tiled bathroom floor,

squares of black and white, in the house where
we first vined together but could not root down.

An exotic game of strategy and chance with no victory
and no loss. O Pattern! O Space! O Movement for

Movement's Sake! If I do other than abstract you,
if I align hand and eye to trace your form and being,

I obscure you so that even the most exact sketch fades
into a kind of death. You are as you are, not as I figure

you to be. To see outside the dimensions of my want,
I have to draw you, shape and line, out of the picture.

ARTIFACTS

After a Saturday in cleaned-up Chelsea, galleries
                 & a bookstore—Naomi alone upriver
with the boys—Midtown's proud
                 sun-blotting canyons ebb behind me,
their ridges turned to skyline. The train I'm riding
                 makes every stop & parallels
a Hudson swollen by days of rain.

             North of Greystone, we flash by two heron,
balanced on obsolete pilings,
                 patient for yellow perch to show
near the surface. Across the river from the birds,
             on the Jersey side, the Palisades' basalt cliffs
stand like the triumphant walls a megalomaniacal king
                 spent all the population of his dominion
to build. In places these tracks come within feet
                 of the brackish, high-tide Hudson:

I've often wondered how long before a flood
                 or the water's steady, cyclic rise erodes
the ballast bed & sinks these rails to artifacts.
             Just below Tarrytown where as with all stations
we won't stay long,
                 the old Tappan Zee looms into view,
mostly torn down, only two spans left rising
                 from the river, two spans severed
from each other & unmoored from either shore.

             Beyond here, the Palisades look less a fortress
& more a leviathan breaching skyward
                 to crash down onto the ship hunting it.
At home, I'll color pages or throw a ball
                 or wrestle with my sons & then cook dinner
with Naomi. We'll eat & talk & hear the stories

of our days. After the boys are in bed, I'll step
onto the porch & in spring's long, thawing light,

I'll look down a hill—cut by water
    coursing through time—to where the high school,
its Gothic Revival brick, will block my view
      of the valley & I will not be able to see as far
as the river, will not be able to see as far as the other side,
    where cliffs jut above the water, igneous & hard.
Igneous & hard. Though I have tried,
         I cannot make this world
into what I want it to be.

[WEATHER OF SUMMER AND WEEKEND BLUR]

Weather of summer and weekend blur
in my three-year California boyhood.

The park at Malibu Creek this afternoon
could be July or Saturday.
        Dad
marches us to a stagnant pool, film setting
of forgettable *Tarzan* sequels, the great White
colonial fantasy splashing with his monkey
or Jane.
    The news has been harping
on cougar-mauled hikers in the coastal hills
California calls mountains.
         Trooping back
from the pool, I ask if I'm safe
         from (lurking
and camouflaged)
      in the high, dry grass.

Of course I am.
     In the picnic ground, we unpack
lunch (peanut butter, forgettable).
          As we eat,
the hills above us are quiet—high and dry dead.

Then, a riot of fire trucks heads upslope,
wailing amplified among the inclines.
         When their siren-
whine has passed, the yip-howl of coyotes.
           Staccato.
Every ridge anxious with it.
        Rising and falling
with it.
   The dead (high, dry) hills yip-howl alive.

Rise and fall. Lurking.
        Alive.

                Me, safe?
                      Of course?
And the day affixes,
        sphinx moth pinned
in the vitrine of specimens
                I cannot uncollect:

Malibu Creek, July or Saturday.
              Tarzan and (lurking)
cougars in the grass.
                And the dead hills
(high, dry) alive with rise and fall.
            Staccato.
Anxious.
    Then always now: (lurking) above me
(coyote, coyote, coyote) the hills yip-howl alive.

NOT A PRAYERFUL KNEELING (FOR JOHN LEWIS)

I bought a children's book, on the day you died,
about Muddy Waters.

When I cashed out, behind me on a cushioned bench,
the owner's dog slept.

A springer spaniel named Virginia, the state where
generations of my people

worked tobacco rows or buffed silver
in plantation houses.

Next morning, I read the book to my youngest
when he woke up early.

He had wet the bed & called for me
& not for his mother.

After we had breakfast, he watched a cartoon
& I opened *The Times*.

I read the headline that reported your death
but could not read the article.

Later that morning, as I folded laundry, my youngest
dawdled into the room.

I played him a Muddy Waters album. In "Mannish Boy"
when he throats out *oh, yeah*

and makes it last for a dust-thick summer afternoon,
Muddy rolls desperation

into the inextinguishable will to keep on living,
a dual state of being

I have only recently begun to understand.
I read the article

after I told Naomi you had died & she asked,
How did he die?

She meant *how could* he *die*, myth we were raised on,
Freedom Riding & Selma.

I read enough to answer her stated question & saw you
in a photo kneeling.

This was not a prayerful kneeling, though your head
was bent groundward.

A state trooper had his hand on your shoulder
& his billy club raised

to hit you, again, in the ribs or head. I could not
look away to finish reading.

As on many Saturdays, I jogged in Nelson Park
on the day I read you had died.

The morning was so hot—no Alabama broil
but hot for along the Hudson—

that only five other people were in the park.
Under a flaming copper beech,

a Black woman sat on an aluminum bench,
talking on her phone.

Across the field, in the shade of a plane tree, two men,
a couple, lay on a blanket

& talked face to face. A White man practiced layups
at the basketball court's far hoop.

At the near, a light-skinned boy took foul-line jumpers,
trails of his long, fine hair

undulating each time his sneakers landed on the court.
I don't know why

I'm telling you all this. I must be afraid. One day,
in person or metaphor,

hymns meant to calm my nerves will hum in the warming,
pre-magnolia air. I will be walking

straight toward a wall of callused hands gripping hardwood
and waiting down the road.

Out across the highway, the Mattress & Awning Store
will be closed for the day.

When I come closer to the wall, my song will drop
to a lowdown gravel

& dust moan, wide & flat as any delta. *Turn Back
Turn Back Turn Back*

will shock between my synapses, will thrum & surge
along my arteries.

Survival will seem sweet. How will I walk then
into the wall, the hands,

the hardwood? How will I give myself up
to be cracked open?

How will I bend my knee, bow my head to the road,
& accept the splitting

of me, the splitting of me until I am spilling,
until I am spilled?

FOR I THINK UPON THE PRICE OF MY REDEMPTION

True, the only capacity for belief
remaining in me is faith
in each planetary spin unspooling day
into next day,
           next day when my body
sweats to make risen bread, bread eaten
in continuance
           of my risen body.
                      I do admit:
    I think often of escape,
               wandering
into the desert,
           lying like a wadi in wait
of heavy rain,
           my prideful flesh
redolent of sun,
            absent of responsibility.
(The failed colonist's dream
                more alive in me
than I'd confess
           to any ear but yours.)

I do not go. Sudden storm and deep
cold. Rotted pillar and caving roof.

I stay and am redeemed by forfeiting
wages of sin that could have thrilled
along my tautening skin. Always,

I stay to be at the table with you.
For the next day. And the next day.

At the table with you, my body
beyond this risen bread. With you,

my bread beyond this doubting body.

ON A DIFFERENT DAY

On a different day, I'd see
the cormorants resting
on these moldering pilings
as sign of the once and future ruin
surrounding me always.
                        On this day
I take joy in the ebb and flow
that I both know and cannot know:
cormorants perch where earlier
a woman wanting to know the rhythm
of tidal water launched her rowboat
into Manursing Lake.
                        On some future
day, perhaps this water will crest over
the trail and no one will stand
where I stand now.
                        No death to all this,
just some life become other life.
                        On this day,
the sodden wood of a ruined dock wastes
more away and a quartet of cormorants
scans the reeds in the nearby salt marsh.

And the saline air calms my lungs.

And behind me the high-tide Sound
lambasting the rock-strewn shore
of the Point seems an abstract rumble.

And, for today, I want
no more purpose
than this.

5. MYTHOLOGIES OF THE SUBURBS

THESE AND ALL ELSE WERE TO ME THE SAME AS THEY ARE TO YOU

When, on a city map,
                                         the newspaper plotted
                    all the murders
during the first summer
                          I lived in Philly,
red dots eclipsed
               Point Breeze
                         and Kensington,
           seeped
      across Elmwood Park,
                   Strawberry Mansion,
         Nicetown.
                          Red dots in a scatter chart
     circled around
           the towers of Center City
                        because the paper,
measuring in column inches,
             could not expend
                      language
to keep pace
         with the killing.
                   Which is to say,
     many Black boys
             died
that summer with not
           a public whisper
of their names.
          Last week,
               an old colleague
        wrote to say
one of my first students,
           a White boy
    grown into a White man,

                    absorbed more opioids
                                        than his body
could withstand,
                died cold and glassy-eyed.
I have seen no hard fact,
                        no record of this
with article and headline,
                                    not for days now.
            If the same paper
plotted
            this season's fentanyl dead
                                would dots
        enshroud every city
                    in Pennsylvania?
                When I have said,
What about the Blacks boys,
                        I have meant: when we could not
let ourselves hear
                as one child howled
                                in the yawning desert,
            when we left one child
bleeding in the street,
                        we opened for any
                mother's child
                            a possible world
        of pinpoint pupils
                        and lonely, sidewalk death.
                When I have said,
What about the Black boys,
                        I have meant: if we disregard
        the branch and fork
                                of any fissure,
            we leave all the grid
of the brick wall
                                        vulnerable to buckle.
                When I have said,
What about the Black boys,
                        I have meant: if I do not stop

to answer—
        above the grinding din

                of small choices and routine—
  my own question,

            I will be left with a red silence.

        I am left

   with a red

silence.

        When I have said,

What about
  the Black boys—

THE DISMANTLING OF MOSCOW'S BELLS

After the Soviets wrested power from the Czar, they campaigned
against churches, repurposed or flattened them, removed their bells,
changing the sound of Moscow and with it the city's sense of time,

the rhythm of its hours and days and seasons.
                                               I would have loved silenced
bells in my boyhood: my family lived up the street from the Presbyterian church,

the town's first house of worship, adjacent to the village green, imposing
and whitewashed.
                   Wherever I was—sitting in classroom rows and columns,

avoiding homework with handfuls of candy behind the gas-station store,
losing a pickup game in my neighbor's driveway—I could hear the Presbyterian
mark the hour.

             For me, that bell tolled with hypocrisy, the town's churches
packed on Sunday while all week I waited for the next bigoted rock to be lobbed:
after gym we're changing in the locker room and this White kid asks,

Why'd the nigger cross the road?
                          He's looking my way and it's a small town
and he knows me and he knows my mother is Black.

                          In my head I answer, *To get away
from dumb hicks like you* while some unhelpful soul responds, *To get fried chicken
on the other side.*

          Neither of us correct: *Who cares, man?*
                               Why didn't you run that nigger over?
When punch lines like that landed and tinny echoes of laughter ricocheted

off the lockers, I promised one day to hit the Thruway and stay gone.
                                                    But here I am,
every summer with my sons, and most Thanksgivings.

                                               I want the boys to know
my mother and father—the lilt and elided aitches of his English, her penchant
for purple in clothing and decoration, his guitars crowding the front room,

her books tumbling down shelves in the study.
                                                 Douglass claimed many more slaves
would have run off if not for the bonds of family.

                                      And I wonder now if any of us
can outrun the landscape of our upbringing.
                                     My younger self wouldn't understand

that idea or my coming back here, would write me off as coward or hypocrite
fit for this town.
                The Presbyterian bells still chime on the hour when we're here,

come ringing up Genesee Street.
                                    While my boys romp between beds of coneflowers
and hellebores in my Black mother's garden that is also my White father's garden,

they can't help but hear what I heard: days divided by clangs that jar at first
but then settle into the undulant hills shadowing the valley until every hour
the bells become what you know of time and home, become what you were

and what you worry is all you can ever be.

LESSONS ENDING IN ALLEGHENY PLUM

The furrows in a brain are called *sulci*.
The capstones to pyramids are called
pyramidion. I, the teacher, learned
all this from my students. I learned too
that adolescents tend not to complete
essays when their fathers are ventilated
and dying. Or, when each day at school
they get called *faggot*. These are not

the lessons I intended to teach or be taught,
but they are the lessons I have for you today.
Tomorrow, I doubt these lessons will change.
Maybe *father* will be *mother*. Maybe the epithet
will be *nigger*. Maybe there will be more of them.
Lessons. And all about as acid as an Allegheny plum.

NOTES TOWARD MY YOUNGER BOY'S POSSIBLE BIOGRAPHIES OF ME

(1) *He was the type of man who hated dogs but once saved a dog's life.* True on both counts. I do hate dogs. So many of them exhibit two qualities I hate in humans (including me): a capacity for viciousness and reflexive loyalty. I did also save a dog's life, but this would be mundane except the boy was four and I was his pedestaled father. We were on one of these morning walks the boy and I used to take when the virus kept us distant from other families and walking might be the only exercise he'd have for the day. We'd loop around neighborhood streets, cut through the parking lot at the old Catholic school turned day care, and then head back up the hill to home. The dog—shaggy, light-brown terrier mutt—was running in the middle of Linden Road and a driver who either didn't see the dog or didn't care if he hit the dog was bearing down. I saw it first in the wideness of the boy's eyes. When I looked up and saw what he was seeing, I knee-jerk called the dog to me. It came trotting long-tongued out of the road and toward me. After sniffing at my hand, it kept to the sidewalk before turning into a driveway and disappearing. *You saved that doggy.* The boy said this in the moment and with enough regularity over the next few months to make me think it had imprinted firmly. Did I actually save the dog? Fair enough. The dog might have felt the wind of the barreling car approaching from behind and veered out of the road. Or the driver might have finally seen the dog or grown a heart and slammed on the brakes, causing a screech and spooking the dog out of the road. Also, I doubt I intended to save the dog for the dog's sake. But even if I could suss out my split-second intent, would it matter? The boy thinks I *saved that doggy* and saved it for selfless reasons, and I'm inclined to let that stand

(2) *He was the type of man who once saved a dog but who was also prone to prolonged fits of rage.* The first claim, as we've seen, is true, or true enough. The second claim is also true. I whirl into anger over wrongs small and large: not being responded to quickly enough (where *quickly enough* equals fewer nanoseconds than amount to three entire seconds) or the police shooting an unresistant Black woman (where *unresistant* equals asleep in her bed at the time). With regularity, I stamp upstairs, slam the door—setting the

house frame to its accustomed rattle and shake—and remain unavailable, sometimes for hours. Never mind trying to talk me out of this temper: I'll spatter and scald, a roux set in a pan over a burner cranked too high. If he is there before I am stamping and gone, I can see myself in the wideness of the boy's eyes. When I look to see some reflection of what he sees, I cannot find in me the dog to beckon out of the road

(3) I can't name the third possibility. Or, I don't want to hazard naming it on the faulty logic that all that is unnamed cannot be true. The possibility goes something like this: in the sunlight, outside the windows to this room, where the boy slept for the first three years of his life before bunking with his older brother, a dogwood (*Cornus florida*) shades the front yard. It is beautiful in the way of all spring plants in this climate, with their narrative of rebirth, their choral efflorescence in the face of a certain end. Even at night, viewed from the sidewalk, the tree is beautiful, light from the day seeming to incandesce out of the whiteness in its branches. From this desk though, once the sun and the boys are down, I can't see the hillside outside the double-hung windows. The angle of the lamplight reflecting off the panes makes the domain beyond them seem an endless darkness, glassy and opaque. I know in my mind, just out there, just out there is the dogwood, its bracts nacreous even under this scant moon. But the bend and trick of light is too much and becomes all I think I can see, until from where I sit in the night—behind this closed door, seeing and not seeing—the flowering dogwood, loses all about it (shade, bract, nacre) that was true, or true enough to keep me in the world and calling out

ON BLACK QUARTERBACKS & DOGFIGHTS IN VIRGINIA WOODS

When he danced in the pit
where boys break boys
& those who survive
become men who break
men, when he soft-shoed,
boogalooed on the clipped grass,
we cheered for him. But back home,
back roads, backwoods, dirt
& Virginia pine, when he made
another thing dance—held it
on a lead while it reared
on hind legs, elevated to *relevé*,
while it strained shoulder & neck
against the leather strap—
when he unleashed it,
& it sped like a hurricane
at its mark, we howled
for the dogs. I howled
for the dogs. For the dogs
I had known, abandoned
in Brewerytown, in high weeds,
in the no-man's-land along
the freight line. Lolling tongues.
Scabrous flanks. Skin at neck
& chest peeled back, open
to red meat. Eyes watery
& vacant as a purpose served,
as the eyes of boys, sitting
at their Monday-morning desks,
having broken other boys,
grasping for what they'd won
& finding it, in the bell-ring
of their minds, already lost.

WARD POUND RIDGE

My older son holds a rotting chunk of fallen birchwood.

He explains that fungi in the chunk of birch turn the wood blue.

Below us, a creek bends blue and north to run in the same direction as the trail.

The creek holds onto a fringe of ice that has not melted in the rare warmth of this day.

Water tumbles from under the fringe and courses over smoothening stones fixed in the creek bed.

For the moment I want to know, from my son and the water, the alchemy and astronomy of all things.

But then, tossing the birch into leaf fall, he sprints along the trail, drops down the slope, and in a moment, is gone

into gray-lit forest I know must be there but cannot see.

MYTHOLOGIES OF THE SUBURBS

The hen arrived in early summer,
origins unknown, pecking at seeds,
insects, fallen mulberries in the yard until
the boys gave her a name: *Boxster the Chicken.*

By midsummer Boxster was a fixture,
appearing at the neighborhood BBQ, gorging
on dropped tortilla chips while above her comb,
on the grill, cooked the sauce-slathered
breast and thigh meat of her kin.

And two weeks after that, the older boy,
waiting to have a catch with me and his brother,
called into the house: *I found Boxster the Chicken
under the bush.* From the backdoor, I could see
the yard covered in white, the grass a massacre
of feathers. The raccoon that killed Boxster tore
off her head, head that we never found. Stripped
the flesh from her breastbone. Left only
splayed wings and scaled, yellow feet. Blowflies
rose from and settled back onto her body,
moving in unison, like a living shadow,
while yellowjackets skimmed the lawn
and landed in sprays of viscid blood.

Boxster had been, if not a pet, the mascot
of our summer, a joke on car trips, a chant
around campfires, a cue in charades. I scanned
each boy for signs of sadness at this death,
proximate and grisly. Each the same: no hint
of grief or revulsion, engrossed and edging
closer, as near as he thought I'd allow.

They stayed enthralled while I removed
Boxster's remains, the younger boy tight
to my right elbow, craning to see. I slid
a grain scoop, snow shovel in winter,
under the rigored corpse and lifted it above
a black plastic bag spread open on the grass.
Holding Boxster aloft, I aimed her carcass
toward the yard bag's open mouth,
tilted the shovel, and dropped her in.

As I knotted the bag closed, the older boy
asked, *Are we going to bury Boxster?* Here will be,
I thought, the point of distress, grief finally
worming past the armor of his fascination.
But when I said, gruff and quick, *No, I'm throwing
the bag in the trash*, he shrugged, handed
a baseball glove to his brother, and tromped
with the younger boy to the yard's far end.

I walked, the bag and Boxster outstretched
in front of me, to the garage where without ritual
I tossed the hen, black-sheathed, into the garbage can
half-full with gray bags of household trash.
Then, unspooling the hose to the forsythia,
I washed the hen's blood from the lawn.

The boys were impatient and bickering
while I looped the hose back onto its rack.
They were ready for me to take up my position
at the near end of the lawn. I arrived there,
and the older boy threw me a baseball—
cowhide stitched over a cork and rubber core—
and for an hour with his brother, we sent
that ball in long arcs back and forth, back
and forth, while at our feet the scattering
of white feathers and the slanting of afternoon
shadows arrayed themselves over the yard
like an augury we did not care to read.

IN SOME AMERICA / A GUN

The pin oak leaves turned maroon,
then dried brown, and in late
autumn, they fell. All winter
I waited for their green return.
Into early spring.
                    They are green now
outside the window on the classroom's
south wall. Greener for the day's clear
blue scrim of sky. Through the east wall's
window, open to mid-spring heat, I can
hear the younger children screeching
on the playing field up the hill.
                        Yesterday /
today / tomorrow / in some America / a gun
in a child's hand has killed / is killing /
will kill / other children.
                        Yesterday,
the killed children were the age
of my youngest child. Today,
they are the age of my oldest.
How old will the children be
tomorrow?
          I imagine their eyes /
late autumn / winter / early spring
dilated with fear. Or, narrow
with no capacity to understand.
The killer's mind a hailstorm
of anger and confusion.
                    I cannot
imagine it.
          I am sitting in a classroom.
The pin oak outside the window
has come back to green. The gun
in the child's hand killed teachers too.

This a teacher's job / yesterday / today / tomorrow/ in some America: to die wrapped in our children. Late autumn / winter / early spring / teachers dead among our children.
                      In some America:
the killer /
        the gun /
                —in the doorway
to her classroom,
          a teacher /
                    —below windows
hung with their wild art,
                    under their small desks,
children /
        how old will they be /
                tomorrow?

6. RENDERS ITSELF VISIBLE IN MY BODY

HERON AND LIGHT AT THE CROTON RIVER

The everyday frustration: I cannot tell you
about the great blue heron, a long elegance,
flashing behind the maples' last yellow,
the oaks' final ochre. Heron, a floating

shadow unlit in November's low sun.
Heron, landing away from the river's eddy
and riffle, in some cold, tranquil pool keeping
its serene, black-crowned vigil. I cannot

tell you this—you are not here. And if you were,
a drift of leaves spiraling just above your head
or the sun in descent glaring into your eyes,
no doubt you'd see the water, the current,

the bird, the wings, the sun, the trees, the trees,
the trees—all of it—in a different diffusion from me.

FREQUENCY & AMPLITUDE: THE CHILD / SING

I have known this volume in my life / I am fluent
in it / "they" heard the man when he instructed
the crowd to, *Please hold your applause until all graduates
have crossed the stage.* "They"—mothers, sisters, aunties,
cousins—ignored him. Willfully. Their child /
on top of the usual high-school bullshit—homework
& hormones—dealt every day with barbed-wire eyes
policing their every movement through the hallways:

should the child be here / is the child smart enough /
if smart enough / quiet & disciplined enough / humble
& low enough / look-you-in-the-eye-and-say-hello enough.
Every day / the child dodged rubber erasers aimed
at her silhouette. Every day the mockery of skin / of lips
& nose / of the body's contours where it rounds the hips.

& a history of hair stories: box braids or locks /
every day / pulled on as if the lead chain to a coffle. Bow
your head & walk this way. / Their child. / They heard *Please hold*
& were loud nevertheless. Erupted. Rattled the rafters. Shook
the White-man portraits lining the wall into the auditorium.
They did what all of us should do: send up / every day /
praise for the child / sing the child's survival / every day /
every day / act a fool until the child is all grin & teeth

& shaking a head in mock embarrassment that is
an acknowledgement of love. An acknowledgement
that whatever broken glass is set into the next wall
to be scaled / when the child's name is called / there will /
always & every day / be a loudness / from the back
joy & bulwark against ruin / joy & bulwark against wrack.

DANSE PRINTEMPS ET QUARANTAINE

Near the end of my run
before the road turns steeply
uphill toward the house, I see
a girl alone on her front lawn.
The day is beautiful, cloudless
& cerulean, the latest in a string
of beautiful days. The girl has wound
her long black hair into a tight bun
& wears brown plastic-framed glasses
not unlike my own & dances.
If she is dancing to music, I can't
hear it. But then I don't listen too intently:
I want her to be dancing to music
only she can hear.
                    I imagine the virus
has kept her out of a studio for months.
I imagine she has danced only
in her basement or to the blue glare
of a computer screen, disconnected
from the other dancers.
                    Besides *plié*,
I do not have the language of dance
to describe the few moves she performs while
I run past. In the last one I catch, a Cubist
discombobulation of limbs, she arches
her back until her hands touch the ground,
then throws each leg separately
over her head in a movement that would,
if I attempted it, break into pieces
my embrittled body.
                    Whatever I become
from here, I always want to be
this girl.
          Dancing—I suppose, yes—

dancing while people are dying.
Not out of callow or callous
indifference. But in celebration
of the dead. Celebration expressed
as survival. Survival expressed
as a clamant act of love, an act
not native only to me but practiced
until it resides in me, muscle & sinew,
an imperfect act that is the only one
I can think to do.
     Dancing.
Dancing, until the imagined company
of dancers spins & bends around me, until
the music others cannot hear renders itself
visible in my body.
       Dancing, until each passerby
believes again in cloudless & cerulean. Again
in this day & the possibility of the next.

NOTES ON THE POEMS

The title "Metaphysics with Poppies" is borrowed from Pablo Neruda's poem "I Explain a Few Things" translated by Galway Kinnell and found in *The FSG Book of 20th-Century Latin American Poetry* (FSG, 2011).

"Deep Down, Every Sinner" is based on the altered photographic prints in Ken Gonzales-Day's *Erased Lynching* series, which I saw at The Racial Imaginary Institute's exhibition at The Kitchen (NYC) in 2018. The epigraph for the poem comes from Toni Morrison's "Black Matters," found in *Playing in the Dark* (Vintage, 1993) and appeared on wall text elsewhere in The Racial Imaginary Institute's exhibition.

The section title "Is You Is" and the poem title "Is You Is, or Is You Ain't? (The Answer Becomes a Set of Further Questions)" borrows from the title of the Billy Austin and Louis Jordan song "Is You Is or Is You Ain't My Baby?" (1943).

The epigraphs to "Of Marks & Lacks" appear in *If Not, Winter: Fragments of Sappho* (Vintage, 2002), Anne Carson's translations of Sappho's poems.

The title "*Turn, hell-hound, turn!*" is borrowed from Act 5, scene 8, line 4 of *Macbeth*.

The title of "*for I think upon the price of my redemption*" is borrowed from the second edition of Augustine's *Confessions*, translated by F.J. Sheed (Hackett, 2006).

The title "*These and all else were to me the same as they are to you*" is borrowed from Walt Whitman's poem "Crossing Brooklyn Ferry."

The title "Mythologies of the Suburbs" is borrowed from Jorge Luis Borges's "Borges and I," translated by Ilan Stavans and found in *The FSG Book of 20th-Century Latin American Poetry* (FSG, 2011).

ACKNOWLEDGMENTS

Thank you to the editors of the publications where the following poems originally appeared, sometimes in earlier drafts and sometimes under a different title:

The American Poetry Review, "A Black Mother's Child Considers His Lost Dream of Immortality" and "Metaphysics with Poppies"
Bennington Review, "[Weather of summer and weekend blur]"
Copper Nickel, "The Dismantling of Moscow's Bells"
Denver Quarterly, "Notes Toward My Younger Boy's Possible Biographies of Me" and "Romanticized Portrait of My Self-Loathing as the Poleman in Eakins's *Rail Shooting on the Delaware, Also Known as Will Schuster & Blackman Going Shooting* (1876)"
Inner Forest Service, "Abrupt Edge"
The Kenyon Review, "Deep Down, Every Sinner"
Kweli, "In Some America / a Gun" and "On Black Quarterbacks & Dogfights in Virginia Woods"
New Plains Review, "*for I think upon the price of my redemption*" and "Weighing Death by Patricide (on the Old Croton Aqueduct Trail)"
The Night Heron Barks, "Is You Is, or Is You Ain't? (The Answer Becomes a Set of Further Questions)"
Massachusetts Review, "Horace Silver Hexagonal Blues" and "Lesson Ending in Allegheny Plum"
Milk Press, "These Moral Currents Cut"
Ovenbird, "Lady Soul"
Poetry Society of America (online), "*Danse Printemps et Quarantaine*"
The Progressive, "All the Possible Bodies"
Quarterly West, "Of Marks & Lacks" (IV.) and "Of Marks & Lacks" (X.)
The Southampton Review, "Ward Pound Ridge," "Selfhood Among Nationhood: Mythic Imperatives," and "Frequency & Amplitude: the Child / Sing"
Tampa Review, "Mythologies of the Suburbs"
Under a Warm Green Linden, "These and all else were to me the same as they are to you"

underbelly, "Of Marks & Lacks" (III.), "Of Marks & Lacks" (VI.), and "Of Marks & Lacks" (VIII.)

The Westchester Review, "Of Marks & Lacks" (I.), "Of Marks & Lacks" (XII.), and "Subject of My Desire (in Which You Do Not Figure)"

I am exceedingly grateful to Amy Vijayanagar for including "On a Different Day" and an excerpt from *"Danse Printemps et Quarantaine"* as part of the Rye Poetry Path in Rye, NY.

Thank you to Sally Bluimis-Dunn for including "Artifacts" in Parley.tv's "Parley Ecopoetry Series: Words to Celebrate the Earth."

Thank you to Indolent Books for including "Not a Prayerful Kneeling (for John Lewis)" in its "Transition: Poems in the Afterglow" series.

As a teenager, I voraciously read the liner notes to hip-hop albums, in which the artists were often voluminous in their acknowledgments. As all artists should be. Please indulge me while I channel the spirit of those bygone liner notes: many people in my life deserve thanks. No art is made in a vacuum. My name is on the cover, but I didn't write this book in isolation. I was buoyed by open-hearted communities and a loving family. Many thanks for the support I've enjoyed over the years:

To friends, teachers, mentors, neighbors, and colleagues from the following communities: New Hartford, Haverford, the Syracuse MFA Program, Cave Canem (forever a brick in the house), Philadelphia, Springside Chestnut Hill, the Solstice MFA Program, Ossining, Rye Country Day, Manhattanville University, and the Manhattanville MFA Program.

To the New York State Council on the Arts and the New York Foundation for the Arts for a 2023 Artist Fellowship in Poetry, which provided funding while I was finishing this collection.

To the Poetry Society of America and judge Wayne Miller for recognizing a sample of this work with the 2023 Alice Fay Di Castagnola Award—the praise helped me push through and finish the book.

To Amy Hall, owner of Hudson Valley Books for Humanity, for bringing a bookshop to Ossining and for tracking down obscure books on my behalf. And to Janet Kraybill, who works at the bookshop and who along with her husband Adam Rothberg has been a friend for over 20 years.

To the team at Alice James Books—Alyssa, Julia, Emily, Lacey, Gena—for the tireless work in bringing this book to life and helping to spread the word that it exists. And particularly to my editor Carey Salerno—I'm grateful to have an editor who sees my work so clearly, who champions my work, and who has invested so deeply in this stunning family of "Alices."

To the poets who lent their names and praise to the back cover: Sean Thomas Doughtery (who has believed in me since Syracuse and the beginning); Shara McCallum (sister and role model); Afaa Michael Weaver (the poet I most want to be when I grow up).

To the poets and writers whose friendship has been balm and inspiration as I wrote this book: Anastacia-Reneé, Grisel Y. Acosta, Andrés Cerpa, Quintin Collins, Jennifer Franklin, Rachel Eliza Griffiths, Marcus Jackson, Meg Kearney, Nathan McClain, The Squad (Jedediah Berry, Beth Little, Laura Williams McCaffery, and Renée Watson), Emily Pulfer-Terino, Daniel Torday, and Vincent Toro.

To three poets already named but who generously gave me feedback on a draft manuscript of this book and so deserve to be mentioned twice: Andrés Cerpa (who played Tetris with the order of this book and made it into what it was meant to be); Quintin Collins (the student become the teacher whose attentive reading helped me see the work afresh); and Marcus Jackson (who pushed me hard on form in the way only an old homie can).

To the ancestors and the ancestor poets—you found a voice so that I might find a voice. Particularly to Lucille Clifton, who welcomed me in and showed me the way.

To Terrence D. Williams, whom I met accidentally but who inspired me with his infectious joy and his selfless community building. I miss the songs always on your lips and in your heart.

To David B. Eye, who would not let our friendship fall away and whose poems influenced my own. I miss your visits to the house, our trips into the City, and your insouciant humor.

To my oldest friends, Brit Holmberg, Ty Holmberg, Jen Greer Morrissey, and Mike Nashold, whose generosity, humor, and love have for more than 35 years been my compass, have pointed me on my way.

To the friends who through shared experience and through their unconditional love have become family: John Bramlette, Jeff Haines, Isabel Hardy, Dara Newman Histed, Craig Irrgang, Mukul Kanabar, Jeff "Bull" Lezinski, Mark Maggiotto, Chris McCann, Gavin McCarthy, Tim Mulvaney, Andrew Prazar, and Greg Rak. I'm thankful for your wisdom in hard times and your adventurous spirits in good times. I'm also thankful to your families for letting me borrow you some weekends and for also contributing love and support to my life.

To the family I married into and who have never batted an eye at including a wild-haired poet as one of their own: Barry and Alison; Asher, Amanda, and Ameila; Sally; Anna, Charlie, Cici, and Julia; Jeff, Julie, Will, and Kate; and Patrice and Jamie.

To my blood family and the folks they married: Uncle Pete and Aunt Denise; Aunt Joan; Aunt Mary and Uncle Jeremy; Sam, Amanda, and Avery; Elise (who also got the Haley writing genes) and Mark. I wouldn't be the human I am today without the love and joy you've shown me since the day I came into this world.

To Mom, Dad, and Caitlin: your love is at the foundation of my very way of being and of all that I strive to accomplish. Our shared love of learning and books set me on this path and keeps me on it. I admire each of you so deeply. You each have a restless intellect, a desire to build community, and a willingness to fight to make spaces where all people can learn, and these qualities of you inspire my work as a writer and an educator.

To Naomi, Asa, and Isaac: thank you for letting me make art out of our lives. You are my world entire and loving you is my truest poetry. A life without you three in it, ain't no life for me. I love our trips, our talks, the way each of you helps me toward being my best self, your senses of wonder at the beauty in this world, your senses of empathy and justice, and your unique capacities for joy. Each of you should never stop being you.

RECENT TITLES FROM ALICE JAMES BOOKS

Saint Consequence, Michael M. Weinstein
Freeland, Leigh Sugar
Mothersalt, Mia Ayumi Malhotra
When the Horses, Mary Helen Callier
Cold Thief Place, Esther Lin
If Nothing, Matthew Nienow
Zombie Vomit Mad Libs, Duy Đoàn
The Holy & Broken Bliss, Alicia Ostriker
Wish Ave, Alessandra Lynch
Autobiomythography of, Ayokunle Falomo
Old Stranger: Poems, Joan Larkin
I Don't Want To Be Understood, Joshua Jennifer Espinoza
Canandaigua, Donald Revell
In the Days That Followed, Kevin Goodan
Light Me Down: The New & Collected Poems of Jean Valentine, Jean Valentine
Song of My Softening, Omotara James
Theophanies, Sarah Ghazal Ali
Orders of Service, Willie Lee Kinard III
The Dead Peasant's Handbook, Brian Turner
The Goodbye World Poem, Brian Turner
The Wild Delight of Wild Things, Brian Turner
I Am the Most Dangerous Thing, Candace Williams
Burning Like Her Own Planet, Vandana Khanna
Standing in the Forest of Being Alive, Katie Farris
Feast, Ina Cariño
Decade of the Brain: Poems, Janine Joseph
American Treasure, Jill McDonough
We Borrowed Gentleness, J. Estanislao Lopez
Brother Sleep, Aldo Amparán
Sugar Work, Katie Marya
Museum of Objects Burned by the Souls in Purgatory, Jeffrey Thomson
Constellation Route, Matthew Olzmann

ALICE JAMES BOOKS is committed to publishing books that matter. The press was founded in 1973 in Boston, Massachusetts to give women access to publishing. As a cooperative, authors performed the day-to-day undertakings of the press. The press continues to expand and grow from its formative roots, guided by its founding values of access, excellence, inclusivity, and collaboration in publishing. Its mission is to publish books that matter and preserve a place of belonging for poets who inspire us. AJB seeks to broaden our collective interpretation of what constitutes the American poetic voice and is dedicated to helping its artists achieve purposeful engagement with broad audiences and communities nationwide. The press was named for Alice James, sister to William and Henry, whose extraordinary gift for writing went unrecognized during her lifetime.

Designed by Alban Fischer
Printed by Versa Press